STUDY GUIDE

STUDY GUIDE

LIVE AN AUTHENTIC LIFE OF ABUNDANCE, WELLNESS, AND FREEDOM

ANTHONY ONEAL

NELSON
BOOKS
An Imprint of Thomas Nelson

Published in Nashville, Tennessee, by Nelson Books, an imprint of Thomas Nelson. Nelson Books and Thomas Nelson are registered trademarks of HarperCollins Christian Publishing, Inc.

Published in association with The Bindery Agency, www.TheBinderyAgency.com.

Thomas Nelson titles may be purchased in bulk for educational, business, fundraising, or sales promotional use. For information, please email SpecialMarkets@ThomasNelson.com.

Library of Congress Cataloging-in-Publication Data

Names: O'Neal, Anthony author.
Title: Take your seat at the table study guide / Anthony O'Neal.
Description: Nashville, Tennessee : Nelson Books, [2025] | Summary:
    "What's keeping you from taking ownership of your decisions and
    reaching for your dreams? What stands between you and the life God
    wants you to live?"-- Provided by publisher.
Identifiers: LCCN 2024033050 | ISBN 9781400250110 (trade paperback)
Subjects: LCSH: Christian life. | Peace of mind—Religious aspects--
    Christianity. | Well-being--Religious aspects--Christianity.
Classification: LCC BV4501.3 .O475 2025 | DDC 248.4--dc23/eng/20240829
LC record available at https://lccn.loc.gov/2024033050

Printed in the United States of America

24 25 26 27 28 LBC 5 4 3 2 1

CONTENTS

A NOTE FROM ANTHONY

For a good portion of my life, I felt shut out from the decisions that impacted me most. When I visualize this, I imagine a group of people sitting around a table, talking about me, and making plans for my life. But I'm not there—I'm off to the side, passively watching and listening without the chance to contribute. In other words, for much of my life I didn't have a seat at the table of my life. That was a frustrating reality, to say the least.

Have you ever felt that way—like other people or organizations control your time, talents, money, resources, or relationships? Maybe it's your parents. Maybe it's your boss or your company. Maybe it's creditors or bill collectors or elders who always have a strong opinion about who you should be and what you should do.

Have you allowed yourself to be pushed to the side in your own life? "They know what's best." "I don't have a choice." "I don't know what to do." If you've been there in the past or are there now, you know it's a difficult place to be. It's demoralizing. It's challenging. And it's tiring.

You were created to be in control of your life. You were designed for a purpose and built with the tools necessary to pursue that purpose—to set goals, to work hard, and to achieve your dreams. You were designed for a life filled with abundance, wellness, and freedom.

In this study guide we're going to examine what it takes to experience that kind of life. Specifically, we're going to see how to manage your life—what I call your "table"— and the resources you have to not only make a huge impact in your community but to bring you fulfillment, meaning, and purpose. We're going to explore what it means to take your seat at the head of the table.

Anthony O'Neal

HOW TO USE THIS
STUDY GUIDE

In today's world you and I have access to almost unlimited information: books, articles, podcasts, videos. We can access all the facts we desire, all the knowledge we might ever need.

No doubt that's a wonderful blessing. When I need to figure out the details of a specific tax law or learn how to change a filter in my air purifier, I can find the information quickly and efficiently. When I want to find historical information or look up the definition of a word, I can access that knowledge with the click of a mouse.

Unfortunately, when it comes to the most important areas of my life, I need more than information. I need *transformation*. I need to identify what's not working and change things for the better.

That's the goal of this study guide. I haven't written these pages for you to just learn new information. Instead, I've created this resource for you to engage on a deeper level with important themes discussed in *Take Your Seat at the Table*: finding your purpose; discovering not just *what* resources you've received but *why* you've received them; learning to invite others to join you in maximizing your table; and pushing to experience a deeper sense of abundance, wellness, and freedom. Those are the themes you will grapple with—not to learn more information but to apply these themes in ways that create meaningful change.

To help that process, each session will include four basic sections:

- SET THE TABLE: An introduction to the major topics addressed in the session, along with an opening activity to help you start engaging those topics.
- FIRST AND SECOND COURSES: This is the main content. But it's important to note that this is more than just information to learn. These sections offer questions, activities, and assessments to help you incorporate the information within your unique story.
- DESSERT: This section is designed for application. It will help you answer the question, "What steps do I need to take to *apply* this in my life?"

- CLEAN UP: Finally, you will review the major themes and look ahead to what you'll be exploring in the next session.

As you work through the content, remember to be honest with yourself. Answer the questions and assessments based on what's currently true in your life—not what you'd like to be true or what you hope will be true in the future. By engaging with this material in a meaningful way, you'll give yourself a wonderful opportunity to move forward as the head of your table—ready to make a difference in your life, in your family, in your community, and beyond.

THE BASICS OF YOUR TABLE

In this session you will

- gain a better understanding of what your table is and why it matters,
- explore what it means to sit at the head of your table,
- learn the importance of inviting others to join you around your table, and
- work to identify or describe your assignment, which is your calling or purpose in life.

Prior to working through this session, read chapters 1 and 2 in *Take Your Seat at the Table*.

Set the Table

If you're willing, I'd like you to close your eyes and spend a minute thinking about the family table in your childhood home. Maybe you had a big wooden dining room table with lots of chairs. Maybe it was a card table with folding chairs set up in the kitchen. Or maybe it was everyone setting their meals on a coffee table between the couch and the TV.

Whatever your experience was, put yourself back there during a typical meal—a time when all the people in your home gathered in one place to share something and experience something together.

Can you picture it? Good.

Now see if you can draw it. I'm not asking you to be an artist—just a quick sketch. Use the box to capture what that table looked like and who was there for a typical meal. (Don't worry about drawing people if you don't want to— just use an *X* labeled with a name to show where each person would sit.)

I want you to connect with your table from the past because it serves as a helpful illustration for your table in the present. Not the table where you currently eat your meals. I'm talking about a much different (and much more important) table that encompasses who you were created to be and what you were created to achieve.

In session 1 our goal is to explore what the table represents and what it means for you to take your rightful place at the head.

First Course: Your Table Has Two Main Parts

When I talk about your *table*, I'm talking about your life. Specifically, your table includes everything you've been given by your Creator. That sounds like a lot, and in some ways it is. But all the separate elements can be sifted into two main categories: the resources that make up our table and the people who help us manage our table.

Let's start with the resources. Your table includes everything you've been given to manage within the boundaries of your life. This includes your body and your physical health, your mind and your mental health, your spirit, your most important relationships, your work or career, your finances, your time, your talents, and more.

Use the following questions to gain a deeper look at everything comprising your specific table.

What are the most important characteristics when it comes to your physical body? What do you like best about yourself?

_____

_____

_____

_____

_____

When it comes to your mental and emotional health, what strengths do you bring to the table?

_____

_____

_____

_____

_____

What are your biggest skills, abilities, or natural talents?

_____

_____

_____

_____

Who are the most important people in your life—those you are closest to?

_____

_____

_____

_____

_____

What words describe your spiritual life in recent months?

_____

_____

_____

_____

What are your main financial assets?

_____

_____

_____

_____

_____

_____

All these different elements come together to make up your table. These are all resources you've been entrusted to manage as you operate your life.

But that's not all. The second category included with your table involves the people in your life who participate by helping you manage those resources. Here's a principle: *You should never sit alone at the table of your life.* We all need other people to help us live our best lives and achieve what we've been called to achieve. These people are not included in the makeup of your table. Instead, they sit *around* your table and help you manage your most important resources.

So who are those people in your life? Who is currently sitting around your table?

Look back at the list you made of your most important people. Which of these are contributors and bring something to your table that improves it or helps it grow?

_____

_____

_____

_____

Which of these people subtract from your table and make it harder for you to manage your life well?

_____

_____

_____

_____

We're going to take a deeper look at the importance of gathering the right people around your table in later sessions. For now, let's remember that your table is made up of all the resources and assets you've been given to manage. Your table also includes the people you intentionally invite to help you maximize those resources.

Second Course: Your Place Is at the Head

To reach for abundance, wellness, and freedom, you need to take an active role in determining the course of your life. In other words, you need to have a seat at the table—but not just any seat.

You are meant to sit at the head of your table, which means you are meant to be the primary decision-maker in maximizing your resources and managing the direction of your life. You are called to take control—every person is. Unfortunately, most of us aren't sitting at the head of our table. Most of us don't exercise real authority over our lives and our resources. Instead, we let others tell us what to do; we let others have authority and control over our time and talents and treasure.

Which people have the most influence over how you spend your time? Your money?

_____

_____

_____

_____

Which people have played the biggest role in determining the current direction of your life and the major goals you are working to achieve?

_____

_____

_____

Are you investing your resources in ways that enhance your life and build your table or in ways that benefit other people or organizations?

_____

_____

_____

The big question: Are you currently sitting at the head of your table? Explain your answer.

_____

_____

_____

_____

If your answer to that last question is no, don't be discouraged. Even if you're not sitting at the head of your table right now, you have everything you need to make a change and secure your rightful seat. Here are three steps you can take to accomplish that switch.

STEP 1: REMOVE ANYONE WHO DOESN'T BELONG. This is an uncomfortable step for most people, but it's necessary. To truly take control of your life, you need to de-platform anyone who has been illegitimately operating at the head of the table.

> How do you move a person from the head to a more appropriate place at your table? By setting boundaries. For example, you could say, "I am comfortable with this, but I am not comfortable with that." Or "I am willing to take these steps, but I am not willing to take those steps." Or "I respect your authority and guidance in this area of my life, but your authority does not extend to that area of my life."
>
> Boundaries are a wonderful expression of freedom. And boundaries are one of the primary ways you can assert your authority as the head of your table.
>
> —Anthony O'Neal,
> *Take Your Seat at the Table*, pages 34–35

STEP 2: ASSESS YOUR RESOURCES. As you regain your seat at the head of your table, you'll want to get a sense of the condition of that table. What's working well? What's not? What are the strengths of your table, and what weaknesses are present?

Use the following assessments to help you make those evaluations.

Do you currently have enough time to accomplish everything you need to accomplish, or do you often rush to get things done?

1	2	3	4	5	6	7	8	9	10

[No time]   [Ample time]

How would you score your physical health right now?

1	2	3	4	5	6	7	8	9	10

[Unhealthy]   [Healthy]

How would you score your mental and emotional health?

1	2	3	4	5	6	7	8	9	10

[Unhealthy]   [Healthy]

How would you rate your spiritual life over the past six months?

1	2	3	4	5	6	7	8	9	10

[Weak]   [Strong]

How strong is your financial position right now?

1	2	3	4	5	6	7	8	9	10

[Weak]   [Strong]

How many of your close relationships are healthy and help you achieve your goals?

1	2	3	4	5	6	7	8	9	10

[None of them]   [All of them]

STEP 3: INVITE OTHERS WHO CAN HELP. Remember, you shouldn't try to manage your table by yourself. Yes, you need to exercise authority over your life, but you still need others to help productively manage the resources at your table.

What kind of people should you invite to take a seat at your table? First, invite those who are healthy and will be able to contribute to your goals rather than pull you away from them. Second, look for people who align with your vision and values, who understand what you want to achieve and are excited to help you get there. Finally, invite people who will bring knowledge, experience, connections, and other resources that you don't have. Choose people who will help you fill in some gaps.

What are some gaps in your table that need filling? What do you need that you currently don't have?

_____

_____

_____

_____

_____

_____

Who comes to mind as good candidates for filling those gaps?

_____

_____

_____

_____

_____

_____

What steps do you need to take to invite those people to step into an active role in your life and your future?

_____

_____

_____

_____

_____

_____

_____

Dessert

Here's a question worth considering: Why do you have a table? Why do any of us have a table? What's the purpose behind each of us receiving a collection of resources and connections with other people? What are we supposed to do with everything we've been given?

For decades now our culture has been telling us that the only purpose for our lives is to enjoy ourselves until we die. "Chase your dreams." "Follow your heart." "You only live once." We've been sold the lie that the most important thing we can do is invest in ourselves and in our own happiness—and maybe do something nice or charitable every now and then because that will make us feel good too.

This is a destructive way of thinking. The reality is that you and I are created beings. We were designed *on purpose* and *for a purpose*. Everything we have received as part of our table—our resources, our time, our talents, our relationships, and more—is given to us so that we can use it toward that purpose.

You and I were created to experience abundance, wellness, and freedom. I believe that in my core. But we were also created to help others experience abundance, wellness, and freedom. We've been equipped with specific tools to make a real difference in the lives of others—starting in our families and then working out into our communities and countries.

I call this our *assignment.*

> Remember, your table is your life—everything you've been given during your time here on earth. And the reason you've been given that table is to help you carry out your unique assignment. Your mission. Your purpose. Being a good steward of your table means maximizing all your resources in a way that brings meaning to your life *and* makes a difference in the lives of others *and* improves your corner of the world.
>
> —Anthony O'Neal,
> *Take Your Seat at the Table*, page 12

As we wrap up this session, take a moment to think about your own assignment. What have you been called to do?

To the best of your ability, how would you describe your assignment? What have you been called to accomplish with your table?

_____

_____

_____

Think back to your natural skills and talents—those gifts you received at birth. How do they contribute toward your assignment (or what can they tell you about identifying your assignment)?

_____

_____

_____

_____

_____

Which people in your life are most beneficial in helping you carry out your assignment?

_____

_____

_____

_____

_____

_____

Clean Up

Key points to remember:

- Your table is your life. It includes all the resources you've been given to steward.
- Nobody is able to manage their table alone. You need people who can help maximize your resources and fulfill your assignment.
- It's necessary for you to sit at the head of your table. That means taking control of your life for better or worse.
- You've been given your table to help complete your assignment, which is your unique mission or purpose.

Note: The next session, "The Foundation for Your Table," will explore the themes of spiritual health and relationships. Be sure to read chapters 3 and 8 in *Take Your Seat at the Table*.

THE FOUNDATION FOR YOUR TABLE

In this session you will

- identify why your spiritual life is a key foundation of your table,
- learn why it's necessary to seek spiritual power and resources rather than rely on your own strength,
- explore how relationships with other people become a resource that needs to be managed well, and
- assess how different parts of your life contribute to or pull you away from your God-given assignment.

Prior to working through this session, read chapters 3 and 8 in *Take Your Seat at the Table*.

Set the Table

Wherever you are currently, take a look around and find some foundations. If you're sitting in a chair, for example, look for the foundation of that chair: the legs or the wheels. If you are near a table or a desk, look down to see what keeps that structure standing strong. You might even take a walk outside and see what foundation is holding up your building.

In these cases you're observing physical foundations of physical objects. By *physical* I mean objects you can see, feel, and touch—things that have mass.

But you don't have a physical foundation for the table of your life. Instead, as we'll discover in this session, the foundation of your life is mainly spiritual and relational. It includes your relationship with your Creator and your relationships with other people. Take a moment to process those relationships by answering the following questions.

What words describe what your relationship with God was like during the following seasons of your life?

AS A CHILD:

AS A TEENAGER:

TEN YEARS AGO:

TODAY:

How has your connection with God grown or changed in recent years?

_____

_____

_____

_____

_____

_____

_____

First Course: Your Spiritual Foundation

The primary source or foundation for your success is not your intelligence. It's not your job or career. It's not your bank account or your ability to make friends or whatever letters come up next to your name on the Myers–Briggs assessment. Those things are important *in* your life, but they aren't the foundation *for* your life.

Instead, your life (your table) has a spiritual foundation. You received all the elements that make up your table—your body, your brain, your financial resources, your personality, your time, your work. All these are gifts from your Creator. For that reason your Creator is the foundation for everything you are and everything you do.

This points to the concept of your assignment, which we discussed in the previous session. As a reminder, your assignment is your mission or purpose in life. It's the reason you're here, and the reason you've been given a table. You have a calling to positively impact the lives of others, and fulfilling that calling is the best way to experience abundance, wellness, and freedom.

Take a moment to review what you wrote down about your assignment in the previous session on pages 17–18. Now that you've had time to reflect, is there anything you would change or add when it comes to describing your life's assignment?

_____

_____

_____

_____

_____

_____

What makes you feel most excited about your assignment? Why?

_____

_____

_____

_____

_____

_____

Next, let's think about *alignment*:

> Having a healthy relationship with God means being aligned with God's plan for your life. God created you for a reason, for a specific purpose, which means you will experience the most joy and fulfillment when you live in a way that matches your purpose. But when your choices or your goals pull you away from that purpose, you won't be spiritually healthy. You won't have a meaningful life no matter what kind of salary or other outward sign of success you achieve.
>
> So living in alignment with God is crucial to the success of your table. It's crucial to the success of your life.
>
> —Anthony O'Neal,
> *Take Your Seat at the Table*, page 46

Living in alignment with your Creator doesn't mean your life will be perfect. It doesn't mean you'll stop having problems or that all your dreams will automatically come true. But living in alignment *does* mean you can experience peace and joy even during difficult seasons. And it *does* mean you will have the wind at your back as you pursue abundance, wellness, and freedom.

So how do we achieve that kind of alignment? How do we make sure our choices and goals line up well with the ways our Creator has called us and equipped us? That's not something we can make happen through our own brainpower or willpower. Instead, we need spiritual power.

Jesus told us, "I am the vine; you are the branches. If you remain in me and I in you, you will bear much fruit; apart from me you can do nothing" (John 15:5). We need God's power in our lives. He's already given us everything that makes up our table; therefore, we need Him to help us move in the right direction and make the right decisions. We need Him to keep us aligned with our mission and purpose.

When have you recently reached out to God and asked for help or guidance? What happened next?

_____

_____

_____

_____

_____

_____

_____

How can you identify when you're trying to provide all the fuel and power for your life rather than relying on God? What are symptoms that pop up when this happens?

_____

_____

_____

_____

_____

_____

Second Course: Your Relational Foundation

When I say *relationships*, I'm talking about all your relationships. That includes your most distant acquaintances and your closest friends. That includes your coworkers, neighbors, gym buddies, teachers, coaches, and more. And that certainly includes all your family members, from your great-grandparents to your spouse.

Just like your time and your money are resources within your table, the same is true for all of those relationships. That may sound strange, but it's important: Your relationships are a resource. Which means they need to be managed—and managed well.

Which of your relationships take up most of your time and energy? Which ones require the most from you?

_____

_____

_____

_____

_____

Which of your current relationships help you grow and mature in your relationship with God?

_____

_____

_____

_____

_____

In addition to your relationships being *part* of your table, those relationships are also the *point* of your table. Meaning, relationships are one of the main reasons we have a table in the first place. You and I haven't been given our resources so that we can make ourselves as happy or as comfortable as possible. Instead, we are called to make an impact in the lives of others.

That starts with our families. Our assignment includes doing everything we can to help our spouse, children, parents, and other extended family members reach toward abundance, wellness, and freedom. We're also called by our Creator to make a difference in our communities, our nation, and the world at large.

Doing a good job of stewarding (or managing) your relationships also means learning from the people in your life. Your friends, family members, coworkers, and acquaintances have all seen things and experienced things you weren't able to see or experience, which means they've learned things you don't currently know. Take opportunities to grow and improve on your own journey toward abundance, wealth, and freedom by asking them questions and listening to their stories.

In your own words, what does it look like to steward your relationships well?

_____

_____

_____

_____

_____

_____

In what areas of your life do you currently need help or new information? Which of your relationships could assist you in finding what you need?

_____

_____

_____

_____

_____

_____

_____

Dessert

Each of us has an assignment from our Creator—a purpose or calling that defines our lives. That leads to an important principle: We can't fulfill our assignment when we're out of alignment. In other words, we can't do what our Creator designed us to do when we're not connected with Him through a genuine relationship.

Is it possible you may be out of alignment *with* God, making it impossible to fulfill your assignment *from* God?

Use the following assessments to think that through.

For the final time (I promise), try to state your assignment in a single sentence. What have you been called to do? What is your mission?

_____

_____

_____

_____

_____

_____

Using the following scale, how well does the way you manage your spiritual life line up with that assignment?

1   2   3   4   5   6   7   8   9   10

[Not well]   [Very well]

How well does the way you spend your money line up with that assignment?

1   2   3   4   5   6   7   8   9   10

[Not well]   [Very well]

How well does the way you spend your time line up with that assignment?

1   2   3   4   5   6   7   8   9   10

[Not well]   [Very well]

How well does the way you manage your most important relationships line up with that assignment?

1   2   3   4   5   6   7   8   9   10

[Not well]   [Very well]

Which habits or parts of your lifestyle contribute to your assignment? What are the big parts of your life that push you toward fulfilling it?

_____

_____

_____

_____

_____

_____

Which habits or parts of your lifestyle pull you away from your assignment? What makes it harder to do what you've been called to do?

_____

_____

_____

_____

_____

_____

_____

Clean Up

Key points to remember:

- Your spiritual life is a critical foundation for your table because everything that makes up your table was given to you by your Creator.
- If you are out of alignment with God, you will not be able to fulfill your assignment in any meaningful way.
- Your relationships are part of your table, which means they are resources you have been called to steward well.
- Part of managing those relationships is choosing to learn from the people in your life who can teach you.

Note: The next session, "Mind and Matter," will explore the themes of physical and mental health. Be sure to read chapters 4 and 5 in *Take Your Seat at the Table*.

MIND AND MATTER

I n this session, you will

- explore the importance of your mind and mental health as part of your table,
- explore the importance of your body and physical health as part of your table,
- learn why it's necessary to invite others to your table who can help you invest in your mental and physical well-being, and
- spend time assessing your current lifestyle and its effect on your health.

Prior to working through this session, read chapters 4 and 5 in *Take Your Seat at the Table*.

Set the Table

Do you want to experience something wild? See if you can read this paragraph:

Yuor nubemr one asest is not yuor menoy. Yuor nubemr one asest is not yuor soupse. It's not yuor hmoe or yuor car or yuor 401(k) or aythnig else you can see or tuoch. Yuor nubemr one asest is yuor mnid.

This is a crazy truth about how we are wired as human beings. Our brains are so powerful and so adaptable that they can unscramble words on the fly, as long as the first and last letters are in the right place and all the correct letters are there. This is true not just with words but with whole sentences and paragraphs!

If you weren't able to read the scrambled paragraph above, try again. This time don't focus on the specific letters, and don't try to unscramble each letter one by one. Instead, take a softer look at the words as a whole, and allow your brain to float the correct words and phrases up to the top of your mind.

Crazy, right?

So far in this study guide we've explored the basic elements of your table. We've seen that your table is all the parts of your life that you've been given to steward—to manage. We've seen that you were created to sit at the head of your table, which means taking charge of your life and the management of those resources. And we've started exploring your spiritual life and your relationships as foundational elements.

In this session we're going to focus on two more critical pieces of your table: your mental health and physical health. Let's use a quick assessment to get started. Use the circles to draw a face that expresses your feelings about your current state of mental health and physical health. Again, don't feel pressure to be an artist. If you feel happy or joyful about your current health, you can draw a big smiley face. If not, draw something that expresses how you feel about yourself mentally and physically.

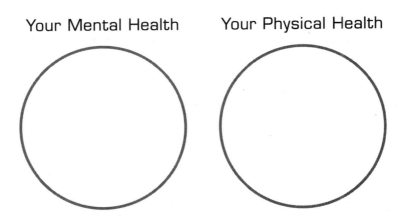

Your Mental Health   Your Physical Health

First Course: Mental Health

As I stated in the scrambled-up paragraph above, your mind is your number one asset. Not your money or your house or your career or even your closest relationships. All those things are critically important, but none will benefit you or your table if your mind gives out.

For that reason I often tell young entrepreneurs to *mind your business, because your mind is your business.*

> The reason I make such a big deal about mental health is because your mind determines the quality and caliber of your table. Whatever plans you have for maximizing your resources, maturing as a person, and making progress toward your specific assignment in life—it all starts with your mind. It all starts with your ability to think and dream and mentally navigate the complexities of life.
>
> —Anthony O'Neal,
> *Take Your Seat at the Table*, page 70

The first step in stewarding your mind is making sure you have everything you need to maintain your mental health—and getting rid of things that negatively affect it. Emphasize the good and get rid of the bad.

What steps are you currently taking to manage and maintain the health of your mind?

_____

_____

_____

_____

What steps would you like to take to improve or support your mental health?

_____

_____

_____

_____

What obstacles are hindering or preventing you from taking those steps?

_____

_____

_____

_____

In earlier sessions we saw the value of bringing other people around your table to help you manage and steward your resources. These should be people who understand your assignment, connect with you on a relational level, and have something they can offer to help maximize your table.

In my opinion, one of the very best choices you can make when seeking a life of abundance, wellness, and freedom is to invite a therapist or counselor to join you at your table. I understand that a lot of people have hang-ups when it comes to getting therapy or going to a counselor. Taking that step can be viewed with stigma. But it shouldn't be. Actually, the opposite should be true! Whatever resources you invest into strengthening your mind and developing your mental health will pay off major dividends in the long run.

On an emotional level, how do you respond or react to the idea of seeing a therapist? How does that idea make you feel inside?

_____

_____

_____

_____

Who in your life has benefited from seeing a counselor or a therapist?

_____

_____

_____

_____

_____

_____

If you were to consider investing in therapy as a way of maintaining your mental health, what are the first steps you would take? What obstacles would you need to overcome or remove?

_____

_____

_____

_____

_____

_____

Whether or not you take advantage of the benefits offered by therapy, all of us need people in our lives who will provide a listening ear and a truthful tongue. We need people who will listen to what we have to say, allowing us to express ourselves honestly and authentically. Then we need at least one or two people willing to tell us the truth—even when it hurts.

To bring those people to our tables we need to actively invite them. We need to say, "I give you space and a place to speak truth into my life whenever you think I need to hear it—and especially if I *don't* want to hear it."

Who among your friends, family members, or coworkers does a good job of listening without dumping on you or offering unwanted advice?

_____

_____

_____

_____

_____

_____

_____

Who can tell you the truth even when you don't want to hear it?

_____

_____

_____

_____

Second Course: Physical Health

In the same way that our minds are a huge asset, making the effort to be good stewards of our physical body and health will put us in a great position to fulfill our assignment over the course of our lives. Investing in physical health produces energy, strength, and stamina—all necessary if we want to live meaningful lives.

Unfortunately, many people in America and around the world acknowledge the importance of physical health without actually building a lifestyle that allows them to maintain or improve their physical health. Most of us are unhealthy, undercutting our ability to pursue abundance, wellness, and freedom.

In your mind, what does it mean to be physically healthy? What are characteristics of someone who is physically healthy?

_____

_____

_____

_____

_____

_____

During what season of your life have you felt the most physically healthy? What steps were you taking during that season to maintain your body?

_____

_____

_____

_____

_____

_____

Doing a good job of stewarding your physical health can maximize your ability to fulfill your assignment. You have the energy and strength required to push through obstacles, put in the hard work, and make a difference.

The opposite is also true. When we do a poor job of stewarding our physical health, we will almost certainly limit or impede our ability to fulfill our assignment. For one thing, we will be less effective on a day-to-day basis. Maybe we won't have the stamina or vitality we need to push forward in our work. Or maybe we'll be distracted by sicknesses or other signs of unhealth. Or maybe we'll feel the need to invest time, money, or other resources into gimmicks or fads that make false promises without providing results.

In the long term, the effects of being physically unhealthy become more pronounced and more serious. When we don't take care of our body, our senior years may be severely limited. We may even become a drain on those we care about. And of course we're likely to die sooner when we are physically unwell. We lose valuable years during which we could have made more progress on our assignment and trained up the next generation to continue our legacy.

What are your goals for your physical health over the next five years? Make a list of five targets you would like to reach.

1.

2.

3.

4.

5.

It's important to invite people to your table who can help you maximize your physical health. That may include friends and family members who love you and want to help you stay healthy, like a workout buddy. Those relationships can produce a lot of positive influence and results.

Ultimately it's best to also seek professional assistance and advice regarding your body and your health. I recommend having a reliable doctor as part of your table. You may also benefit from a nutritionist, a physical trainer, a dentist, or other medical professionals.

Yes, all those connections require time, money, and other resources. But if those resources are invested properly in maintaining your physical health, they will produce great results in your life overall.

Which medical professional(s) do you currently see at least once a year? Which do you see more often?

_____

_____

_____

_____

_____

_____

What physical ailments are you currently experiencing that may require you to seek help from a professional?

_____

_____

_____

_____

_____

_____

Dessert

I know this topic of mental and physical health can feel uncomfortable. These are issues we often avoid if we can. But avoiding problems only leads to larger issues in the future. So as we close out this session, I'm inviting you to take a moment and get honest about your health.

Remember, there's nothing accidental about the way we take care of our mind and our body. We each make choices every day that have direct consequences for our well-being—or lack thereof. Take a moment to evaluate some of the ways your choices and lifestyle are impacting your health and vitality.

In general, do you eat in a way that is healthy or unhealthy?

1   2   3   4   5   6   7   8   9   10

[Unhealthy]   [Healthy]

During a typical week, do you get enough sleep at night?

1   2   3   4   5   6   7   8   9   10

[Rarely]   [Often]

During a typical week, do you exercise in a way that raises your heart rate?

1   2   3   4   5   6   7   8   9   10

[Rarely]   [Often]

Do you typically carry a high or low stress load?

1   2   3   4   5   6   7   8   9   10

[High stress]   [Low stress]

In a typical year how often do you see a doctor to help maintain your physical health?

1   2   3   4   5   6   7   8   9   10

[Never]   [Regularly]

In a typical year how often do you see a therapist or counselor to help maintain your mental health?

1   2   3   4   5   6   7   8   9   10

[Never]   [Regularly]

How confident do you feel that the health professionals you visit are helping you make healthier decisions?

1   2   3   4   5   6   7   8   9   10

[Not confident]   [Very confident]

Based on your answers above, what is one step you need to take in the next week to improve your mental or physical health?

_____

_____

_____

_____

Clean Up

Key points to remember:

- Your body and mind are critical elements of your table because they make it possible for you to fulfill your assignment.
- We must be intentional in maintaining our mental and physical health (nothing good will happen by accident).
- We can invest in our mental and physical well-being by establishing a healthy lifestyle.

- Inviting others (including professionals) to join us at our table is a great way to help us maintain that healthy lifestyle.

Note: The next session, "Work and Reward," will explore the themes of work and finances. Be sure to read chapters 6 and 7 in *Take Your Seat at the Table*.

WORK AND REWARD

In this session you will

- learn how work (and not only your job or career) fits as an element of your table,
- explore how work can become an unhealthy focus or distract from your assignment,
- learn about money as a critical element of your table, and
- develop a vision for your life (goals) and a vision for your money (budget) that work together to help you fulfill your assignment.

Prior to working through this session, read chapters 6 and 7 in *Take Your Seat at the Table.*

Set the Table

"What do you do?"

It's one of the first questions we ask when we meet someone new. We learn their name. Maybe we ask a few questions about their family or where they live. Then we move to their work. "What do you do?"

There are countless ways to answer that question. Most of the time we talk about our job or the way we earn a living. But as we'll see in this session, the idea of work includes more than just employment. The work we are called to do—the work connected to our assignment—goes way beyond just making money.

In your words, how would you define *work*? What is it?

_____

_____

_____

_____

_____

_____

Using the box, write down everything you might do in a typical week that you would consider work.

Once your list is complete, underline each item that you are paid to do (work that produces income).

Next, draw a circle around the items that you most enjoy doing.

Finally, put an asterisk next to the two items that take up most of your time.

First Course: The Role of Work

One important truth to understand is that your work is not your table. As we've seen in previous sessions, your table corresponds with your life. But your work is just one of the many planks in that table—it's not who you are on the deepest levels.

That's important because many of us base our identity on the work we do. "I'm a carpenter." "I'm an executive." "I'm a salesperson." It's easy to drift into believing that our career is the most important thing about us—the thing that defines us at the core. Thankfully, that's not the case.

Here's a quick definition: Wherever you invest a large part of your waking hours, that's your work. If you have a job you do for thirty-five or fifty or seventy hours every week, that's your work. If you're a full-time student, then learning is your work. If you're a philanthropist who spends your time giving money rather than earning money, then that's your work. And if you take care of your family every day, that is certainly your work as well.

I want to make it clear: The reason your work isn't the same thing as your table is because your table is connected to your God-given assignment—but the work you do may *not* be related to your God-given assignment. In fact, I believe many people have work that is actually a distraction or a detriment when it comes to their assignments. The work they have chosen to do pulls them away from their assignments rather than contributing to their assignments—which is a problem.

—Anthony O'Neal,
Take Your Seat at the Table, pages 103–104

What are aspects of your work that contribute to your
assignment? How do they overlap?

_____

_____

_____

_____

_____

_____

What are aspects of your work that sometimes pull you
away from your assignment or distract you from what's
most important?

_____

_____

_____

_____

_____

_____

Let's take a look at two specific situations that can allow our work to cause problems with our table. The first is when that work gets placed at the head of our table—when the work we do becomes so inflated or so absorbing that it determines the direction of our lives. This can happen when a boss or other authority figure sits at the head of our table and asserts too much authority over our time, attention, and resources. Or it can happen when we start to make plans that prioritize work above the other elements.

Either way, this is a destructive situation. Whether we are being pushed around by supervisors or devolving into workaholism, we'll have a difficult time fulfilling our assignment when our work takes over our table.

The second destructive situation is when our work becomes the foundation of our table. This happens when we are so financially dependent on our job or career that everything in our life has to be adjusted to maintain it. To put it another way, if the best things about your life would be shaken or even crumble if you were to lose your current job, then that job has become the foundation of your table.

Of course, most people will have trouble if they unexpectedly lose a job. However, I've learned that our resources must serve to advance our assignment—not the other way around.

Take a moment to think hypothetically about your situation. What would happen if you lost your primary source of income tomorrow? What impact would that have on your family?

_____

_____

_____

What are possible steps you can take to create more financial security?

_____

_____

_____

In your current situation, do you see any evidence that your work (including your boss) has usurped your place at the head of your table? Explain.

_____

_____

_____

Second Course: The Role of Money

Instead of serving as the head or the foundation of your table, the work you do should contribute to your table. It should contribute to your ability to fulfill your assignment. For most of us, that contribution includes money. So let's talk about it.

Your money is a critical part of your table. In some ways it's like the gas in your car—money makes our tables go (and the lack of money often causes us to stall). That's an important principle: The abundance or scarcity of money will make a huge impact on your life and on the lives of others. Why? Because the presence or lack of money plays a critical role in your ability to fulfill your assignment.

Many people in today's world—and especially in the church—think of money as something unclean, even something gross. They understand they need to earn money and spend money, but they believe their life would be better without it.

In my mind, that's a mistake. Here's why:

As human beings, we live in a world of money. Our society is connected by an uncountable number of financial transactions and interactions that happen every single moment of every day. Buying food. Paying bills. Financing a home. Managing debt from your past decisions. Managing investments to try to make a better future. Interest rates. Mortgage rates. Credit card rates. Gas prices. Inflation. Savings accounts. Checking accounts. Debit cards. Online shopping. Free shipping. Salaries. Bonuses. Hourly wages. Federal taxes. State taxes. Local taxes. Sales taxes. Real estate taxes.

I could keep going, but do you get my point? We live in a world made of money, which means we need to be excellent managers of our finances. We need the ability to manage money well as a key part of our table.

—Anthony O'Neal,
Take Your Seat at the Table, pages 126–127

What words describe your attitude toward money? Are you more pulled toward money or repelled away from it?

_____

_____

_____

_____

_____

_____

How confident do you feel when it comes to navigating a world made of money?

_____

_____

_____

_____

What are some ways you would like to grow in stewarding your money and financial resources?

_____

_____

_____

_____

Discipline is one of the biggest tools we all need when it comes to managing our finances. Every day our culture pushes us to buy stuff we can't afford with money we haven't earned. Debt is a trap that's been polished and presented as a can't-miss opportunity, and it's dragging us down one charge at a time.

What does it look like to steward your table in a disciplined way? Here are five stages I recommend for anyone looking to get started in that process.

STAGE 1: BUDGET TO LIVE BELOW YOUR MEANS. This is the most basic step but also the most critical. When you spend less than you make during a given month and extend that out to a whole year, you will be financially healthy.

STAGE 2: BUILD AN EMERGENCY SAVINGS. Once you've got an effective budget, the next stage is to save up enough money to pay for one month of expenses. By *expenses*, I mean bills you have to pay in a given month— housing, transportation, food, utilities, day care, and so on.

STAGE 3: PAY OFF ALL CONSUMER DEBT. This means pay off every single debt that is not a mortgage on your primary home. That may seem impossible, but folks have been doing it for decades by following the debt snowball method made popular by Dave Ramsey. Start by making the minimum payment on all your debts, but throw any extra money you can at the smallest of those debts. Once that is paid off, add that minimum payment to your next-smallest debt until it is paid off. Then keep rolling forward until all your accounts are closed.

STAGE 4: EXPAND YOUR EMERGENCY SAVINGS. Once you've removed all of your nonmortgage debt, use your excess money each month to save three months' worth of income. The idea here is that if you lost your job, you would have three months to find a new situation without needing to make any changes to your lifestyle.

STAGE 5: MULTIPLY YOUR MONEY. When all your debts are paid and you've got a three-month cushion in the bank, it's time to start using your money to make more money. Invest. Build wealth. Save for retirement. Learn how to do all the things wealthy folks do to stay wealthy—and to pass that wealth down from generation to generation.

Do you consistently spend less than you make each month? If not, what needs to change to do so?

_____

_____

_____

_____

_____

_____

Where do you currently fit into the five stages of financial health listed above? What needs to happen before you can move to the next stage?

_____

_____

_____

_____

_____

Dessert

In addition to discipline, vision is another necessary tool for being a good steward of your finances. Specifically, you need to have a vision for your life and a vision for your money.

Your vision for your life is the collection of goals or plans you want to follow. These are the plateaus you are striving to reach, and they don't have to be focused on finances. For example: "Get married." "Raise three or four children." "Launch my own business before I turn thirty-five." "Invest 10 percent of my income every year for retirement." "Write a novel."

Use the space provided to write down the main goals you see as the vision for your life over the next five, fifteen, and fifty years. Be as specific as possible.

What are the most important goals you want to achieve over the next five years?

_____

_____

_____

_____

_____

What are the most important goals you want to achieve over the next fifteen years?

_____

_____

_____

_____

What are the most important goals you want to achieve over the next fifty years? (Be sure to include plans for your resources and your family after your death.)

_____

_____

_____

_____

_____

Having a vision for your life is important, but that vision likely won't get you very far if you don't have a vision for your money. That's another way to say you need a budget—you need a plan for your money that takes into account what you expect to earn, what you expect to spend, and what you plan to do with the excess.

Your vision for your life needs to line up with your vision for your money. For example, if one of your life goals is to purchase a home, you will need to budget in a way that enables you to save money each month for a down payment. Your two visions must work together for you to reach your goals and fulfill your assignment.

Use the outline on the next page to write out the basic elements of your budget.

EXPECTED EARNINGS EACH MONTH: _____

EXPECTED EXPENDITURES BY CATEGORY

    Mortgage or rent: _____

    Utilities: _____

    Transportation (including car payment, gas, and

        maintenance): _____

    Food (including eating out): _____

    Clothing: _____

    Medical/dental: _____

    Entertainment: _____

    Savings/retirement: _____

    Repayment for loans: _____

    Other expenses: _____

EXPECTED EXCESS EACH MONTH: _____

Where do you see a disconnect between your vision for your life and your vision for your money (budget)?

_____

_____

_____

_____

Clean Up

Key points to remember:

- Your work is not your identity (who you are), nor is it your table (your life).
- Your work is part of your table, which means it should help you pursue and fulfill your God-given assignment.
- To successfully steward your money, you need discipline.
- To successfully steward your money, you also need a vision for your life and a vision for that money.

Note: The next session, "Open and Authentic," will explore the themes of work and finances. Be sure to read chapters 9 and 10 in *Take Your Seat at the Table*.

OPEN AND AUTHENTIC

In this session you will

- learn why it's important to keep your table flexible and expandable,
- explore specific situations in which it may be necessary to stretch or shrink your table,
- engage the importance of managing messy situations and messy conversations in the context of your table, and
- highlight the value of authenticity and the privilege of being yourself.

Prior to working through this session, read chapters 9 and 10 in *Take Your Seat at the Table*.

Set the Table

Strange as it may sound, change is one of the few constants we can count on in our world. No matter who we are or what we do, one thing that stays the same in our lives is the reality that nothing stays the same. Everything changes.

That's certainly the case with our tables. Even when we make detailed plans and set up helpful systems, we need to be aware that things will change. Circumstances will shift. Goals and priorities can drift.

For all those reasons and more, it's important that we keep our tables flexible. Adaptable. Open.

Back in session 1 you drew a picture of what your dining room table looked like as a child. Now use the box to draw a picture of your ideal table—the setup you would make for your current dining area if you had total freedom to arrange it as you wish. Again, don't worry about being an artist; do your best to sketch and label *what* you'd like to see with your ideal table and *who* you'd like to join you there each day.

What are the main ways the table you have now is different from the table you grew up with as a child?

_____

_____

_____

_____

_____

_____

What are the main differences between your current table and your ideal table? What changes would you like to see?

_____

_____

_____

_____

_____

_____

First Course: An Open Table

Even though change is a constant in our world, many of us are still resistant to it. We resent change, and therefore we often resist it. We do everything we can to keep our lives the same so that we can remain comfortable.

That's not good for our tables. Since our tables are our lives and we were designed to grow and expand, it's harmful for us to become stale and stagnant. We are designed to fulfill our assignment, which means we need to continually develop and mature in our understanding of that assignment and our ability to carry it out. More than that, we need to continually gather more resources to fulfill our assignment well.

Here's a principle: A healthy table is one that can expand when necessary.

When is it necessary? you ask. There are two answers. First, you need to expand your table when you are unable to fulfill your assignment with your current resources. You feel called to achieve specific goals, but you don't have the money or the time or the energy or the relationships necessary to achieve them. When that happens, you likely need to make changes that will help you acquire those missing resources.

The second reason you may need to expand your table is when you come to major landmarks in life. When you get married, for example, or have children, change jobs, move to a new area, or suffer a blow to your health (or the health of a loved one). Or you find yourself in an empty nest or retired. All of these will likely require major changes in your table, which means your table needs to be adaptable and flexible.

Do you find it difficult right now to fulfill your calling with the resources you currently have? Explain.

_____

_____

_____

_____

What are major lifestyle landmarks you have experienced in the past ten years?

_____

_____

_____

What are lifestyle landmarks you expect to experience in the next ten years? How will your table need to change as a result?

_____

_____

_____

_____

Your table should be able to expand (and sometimes retract) in terms of the resources you are stewarding—your money, time, physical health, mental health, relationships, and so on. But it's also true that the number of seats around your table should be adjustable.

Remember, we invite people to take a seat at our table because they possess resources, experiences, and wisdom we lack. Having that team join us at our table enables us to maximize our resources and do a better job of pursuing our assignment. It's very helpful to have people join us in that pursuit.

There will come times, however, when you face a problem that nobody at your table can solve—a problem that nobody even knows how to start solving. When you find yourself in that situation, that's a good sign you need to expand the number of seats at your table. You need to reach out and find someone else who can join you and add their expertise.

Similarly, there may be times when you feel there are too many voices. There may be times when the people you've invited can't come to a consensus about what's best for your life or even times when someone no longer seems to have your best interests in mind. In those situations it may be necessary to remove one or more people from your table.

> A moment will come when you need to roll people away from your table. At times you will need to remove people from your table, and you don't want those seats to be bolted to the floor. You want them to roll in easily when needed and then roll out again when that need is no longer there.
>
> What does it look like to remove someone from your table? In my experience, it means being both honest and direct: "Thank you so much for everything you've done to help me with [fill in the blank]. It's been great."
>
> —Anthony O'Neal,
> *Take Your Seat at the Table*, page 184

What's important to remember is that your table should be open and flexible, not closed and rigid. Circumstances change just as much as people, which means you will often need to adapt and adjust.

Are you currently dealing with problems or situations that seem too much for the people currently at your table to solve? If so, who might be able to help you solve the problems?

_____

_____

_____

How many people have you currently invited to join your table who have permission to speak into how you manage your resources and fulfill your assignment? List the names below.

_____

_____

_____

Is this too many people, too few, or just the right amount? Explain.

_____

_____

_____

Second Course: A Messy Table

Most of us like it when our kitchen tables are neat and tidy. We like to keep things clean and organized, and it's often stressful when we have to look at or deal with a mess. Even so, we can't ignore the truth that most meals are messy. When we sit down and actually use our kitchen tables, we risk making a mess that will need to be cleaned up later.

The same is typically true for the tables of our lives. When we use our resources to fulfill our God-given assignment, we are taking the risk that things will get a little messy. Maybe a lot messy. So it's important to be ready.

For example, inviting other people to be part of your table means you'll encounter messy conversations. If the people who advise you do so mainly by agreeing with you all the time, that's not a good sign. You want healthy debate at your table. You want dialogue and conversation. You want people who are willing to speak the truth—but the truth can be messy. Sometimes other people will initiate those messy conversations. Other times you will need to take the bull by the horns and initiate what needs to be said. Either way, those healthy interactions are important for a healthy table.

Mistakes are another important part of a messy table. No matter how many wise and experienced people you invite to your table, you will still make mistakes—sometimes even big ones. That reality is unavoidable. The question is, How will you deal with those mistakes afterward?

I suggest three steps: (1) Own your mistake without running away from your error, (2) apologize to those who were wronged and be specific in your apology, and (3) do not make excuses.

How comfortable do you feel in situations that involve conflict?

1   2   3   4   5   6   7   8   9   10

[Very uncomfortable]   [Very comfortable]

How often do your closest relationships challenge you or speak the truth to you in ways that are uncomfortable?

1   2   3   4   5   6   7   8   9   10

[Rarely]   [Regularly]

How comfortable do you feel initiating conversations that may include conflict or strong emotions?

1   2   3   4   5   6   7   8   9   10

[Very uncomfortable]   [Very comfortable]

How do you typically handle things when you make a mistake?

_____

_____

_____

_____

_____

One of the keys to managing a messy table is to let go of perfection and embrace authenticity. Specifically, let go of the mirage of perfection—the false idea that everything should turn out just how you want it to, and that you can always make the right decisions if you just try your best.

Let go of those lies. Perfection is impossible. But authenticity is wonderful!

What do I mean by *authenticity*? It's the ability to be the person you were created to be. No posturing. No pretending. No trying to figure out what other people expect you to do or think or say. Just you living as you.

One of the most important decisions I ever made in my life was choosing to be Anthony Bernard O'Neal all the time. To be myself and nobody else every minute of every day. I wish I could describe the freedom that has come with that choice—not to mention wellness and abundance.

I want the same for you.

—Anthony O'Neal,
Take Your Seat at the Table, page 203

In your own words, what does it mean to be authentic? What does it look like to live authentically?

_____

_____

_____

_____

_____

_____

Where do you see a connection between being authentic and managing a healthy table?

_____

_____

_____

_____

_____

_____

In what areas of life do you currently feel pulled to be inauthentic—to pretend you are someone else or that you want something else? Why?

_____

_____

_____

_____

_____

_____

_____

Dessert

As you go about the important work of managing your table, including the relationships that surround it, keep in mind that not all of those relationships are permanent. In fact, many of the people you invite to your table should be seasonal rather than perpetual.

Of course, some people should have a permanent place at your table. Your spouse. Your various mentors or closest friends. Your parents, if you choose to invite one or both of them.

But many of the relationships should be flexible. If you're launching a business, you may have an advisor you spend a lot of time with for that first year as the business gets on its feet. But once things are rolling, it's okay to move that advisor to the back of your table—or even to end that official connection. In a similar way, it's possible you may want a long, extended connection with a therapist or counselor. But it's also possible you may need therapy for only a specific season—premarital counseling, for example. Once that season is over, it would be unproductive for that person to retain a regular seat at your table.

On a similar track, you should recognize that the seats at your table have wheels. Those you invite won't always stay in the same place. Sometimes you will need to spend more time and invest more energy with specific individuals to handle specific situations.

If you find yourself in a financial jam, it makes sense to "wheel" your financial advisor closer to the head of the table. If you're working through issues in a close relationship, you might move your financial advisor down the table and make extra space for your counselor or spiritual mentor near the head.

In short, do your best to steward the connections at your table in a way that produces the best outcome for you, for those who are with you, and for your assignment.

Make another quick list of the people who are currently at your table—those you have invited to help you manage your life. Mark the relationships that feel permanent with a *P* and those that feel seasonal with an *S*.

_____

_____

_____

_____

_____

_____

Do any of those connections or relationships feel unnecessary for your current season of life?

_____

_____

_____

_____

_____

_____

What steps have you taken or could you take to be open and honest with those at your table regarding their role?

_____

_____

_____

_____

_____

_____

_____

Clean Up

Key points to remember:

- Your table needs to have room to expand and mature whenever necessary. Keep it open rather than closed.
- Openness is important for the resources that make up your table and the people who join you in managing them.
- The most effective tables are messy tables.
- One of the best gifts you can give yourself is the ability to sit authentically at your table.

ABOUT THE AUTHOR

Anthony O'Neal is the number one national best-selling author of *Debt-Free Degree*, a personal finance expert, and the host of the popular podcast and YouTube show *The Table*. Since 2014 he has challenged cultural norms and equipped millions of people to live a debt-free life, break generational wealth gaps, and build true wealth. He has appeared on *Good Morning America*, *Live with Kelly and Mark*, *Fox and Friends*, *Rachael Ray*, *Tamron Hall*, and CNN and has been featured in *Success Magazine*, MarketWatch, *Bloomberg*, *Black Enterprise*, and GOBankingRates, among others.

In 2023 alone his show received over 18.7 million views and 5.3 million downloads, empowering people to achieve financially successful futures. Anthony is a sought-after, dynamic public speaker, addressing audiences of over forty thousand people. He was recognized in *Black Enterprise*'s 2023 40 Under 40 list and *Success Magazine*'s "25 Personal and Professional Development Influencers to Follow."

Anthony resides in the Washington, DC, suburbs. You can connect with him on Instagram, YouTube, TikTok, Twitter, Facebook, and at AnthonyONeal.com.

THOUGHTS

_____

_____

_____

_____

_____

_____

_____

_____

_____

_____

_____

_____

_____

_____

_____

_____

THOUGHTS

THOUGHTS

THOUGHTS

_____

_____

_____

_____

_____

_____

_____

_____

_____

_____

_____

_____

_____

_____

_____

_____

THOUGHTS

THOUGHTS

_____

_____

_____

_____

_____

_____

_____

_____

_____

_____

_____

_____

_____

_____

_____